Let's Meet
Frederick Douglass

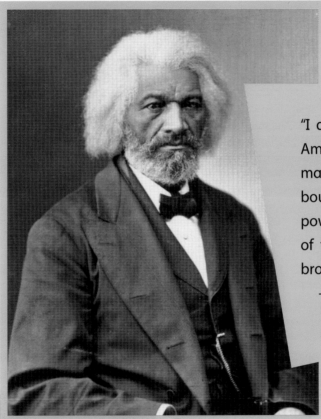

"I am not only an American slave, but a man, and as such, am bound to use my powers for the welfare of the whole human brotherhood."
—Frederick Douglass

Lisa Trumbauer

CHELSEA CLUBHOUSE
An Imprint of Chelsea House Publishers
A Haights Cross Communications Company
Philadelphia

Chelsea Clubhouse books are published by Chelsea House Publishers, a subsidiary of Haights Cross Communications.

A Haights Cross Communications ✦ Company

The Chelsea House World Wide Web address is www.chelseahouse.com

Printed and bound in the United States of America.
9 8 7 6 5 4 3 2 1

Library of Congress Cataloging-in-Publication Data
Trumbauer, Lisa, 1963-
    Let's Meet Frederick Douglass / Lisa Trumbauer.
       p. cm. — (Let's meet biographies)
Summary: Simple text and photographs introduce the life of Frederick Douglass, including his childhood, life as a slave, escape to freedom, founding of a newspaper, public speaking, and public service.
Includes bibliographical references and index.
ISBN 0-7910-7319-X
1. Douglass, Frederick, 1818-1895—Juvenile literature. 2. African American abolitionists—Biography—Juvenile literature. 3. Abolitionists—United States—Biography—Juvenile literature. 4. Antislavery movements—United States—History—19th century—Juvenile literature. [1. Douglass, Frederick, 1818-1895. 2. Slaves. 3. Abolitionists. 4. African Americans—Biography. 5. Antislavery movements.] I. Title. II. Series.
E449.D75T78 2004
973.8'092—dc21   2003004744

Editorial Credits
Gia Marie Garbinsky, editor; Takeshi Takahashi, designer; Mary Englar, photo researcher; Jennifer Krassy Peiler, layout

Content Reviewer
Fredrick A. Morsell, President, FREMARJO Enterprises, Inc.

Photo Credits
©Bettmann/CORBIS: cover, 12, 15, 16, 24; Library of Congress: title page, 21; North Wind Picture Archives: 4, 5, 10, 17; Schomburg Center for Research in Black Culture, New York Public Library, Astor, Lenox and Tilden Foundations: 6, 22; Stock Montage: 7; New York Public Library: 8; Williams College Archives and Special Collections: 9; National Portrait Gallery, Smithsonian Institution/Art Resource: 11; Library of Congress, LC-USZ62-83188: 13; Madison County Historical Society, Oneida, NY: 14; ©The New York Public Library/Art Resource, NY: 18; ©CORBIS: 19; National Park Service, Frederick Douglass National Historic Site: 20, 25; ©Hulton|Archive by Getty Images, Inc.: 23, 29; ©James P. Blair/CORBIS: 26; Sophia Smith Collection/Smith College: 27.

Table of Contents

Young Frederick, Child Slave

Frederick Augustus Washington Bailey was born in February, 1818, in Maryland. He was a slave because his mother was a slave. He was born during a time in America when slavery was legal in Maryland and other southern states. Slaves were not free people. They were treated as property. They were forced to work for their owners.

Frederick Bailey lived with his grandparents in a cabin like this Maryland slave house. Later in his life, he changed his name to Frederick Douglass.

The slaves pictured here work in the fields as Frederick's mother did. She was the only black person in the area who could read. She died when Frederick was 7 years old.

Frederick never knew his father. People said he was white. Frederick's mother, Harriet Bailey, worked long hours in the cornfields. Frederick saw her only four or five times before she died. Frederick lived with his grandparents. He was happy and loved. He didn't realize he was a slave until he was 6 years old. Then he had to live and work on a **plantation** owned by Colonel Edward Lloyd.

Frederick had one brother and five sisters. They probably dressed like these slave children. His brother, Perry, and two sisters, Sarah and Eliza, were also slaves on the Lloyd Plantation.

Aaron Anthony owned Frederick's family and ran the plantation. Slave children on the plantation ate cornmeal mush from a **trough**. They had only one set of clothes to wear. Frederick slept on the dirt floor of a closet. He saw many slaves beaten.

Frederick began to wonder, "Why am I a slave? Why are some people slaves, and others masters?"

Reading, Writing, and Baltimore

Lucretia Auld was Aaron Anthony's daughter. When Frederick was 8 years old, Lucretia sent him to Baltimore, Maryland, to live with her husband's brother, Hugh, and his wife, Sophia.

One day, when Sophia was reading, Frederick asked her to teach him to read. Hugh found out and told Sophia to stop. A slave who could read might find a way to escape.

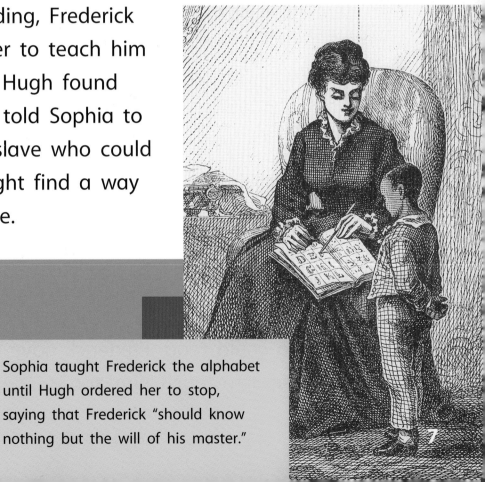

Sophia taught Frederick the alphabet until Hugh ordered her to stop, saying that Frederick "should know nothing but the will of his master."

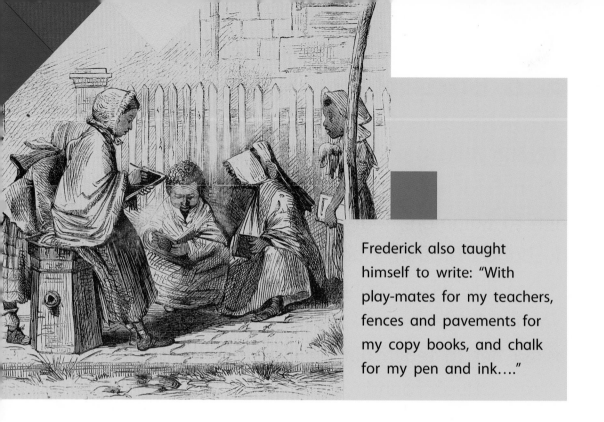

Frederick also taught himself to write: "With play-mates for my teachers, fences and pavements for my copy books, and chalk for my pen and ink…."

It was too late. Frederick had learned the alphabet from Sophia. Now he could learn to read anything. And, if reading led to freedom, Frederick was determined he would learn. He took lessons from anyone who would teach him. On errands for Sophia, he met poor white children who could read. Frederick gave them pieces of bread to teach him, too.

When he was 13 years old, Frederick bought a book of speeches about freedom. The book was called *The Columbian Orator*. He learned words that expressed his feelings about slavery.

He read newspapers and learned about abolitionists—people who wanted to end slavery and who helped slaves escape. He now knew the truth. Every person had the right to freedom.

THE
COLUMBIAN ORATOR:
CONTAINING
A VARIETY OF
Original and Selected PIECES;
TOGETHER WITH
R U L E S;
CALCULATED
To IMPROVE YOUTH AND OTHERS IN THE
ORNAMENTAL AND USEFUL
ART OF ELOQUENCE.

By CALEB BINGHAM, A.M.
Author of The American Preceptor, Young Lady's Accidence, &c.

"CATO cultivated *ELOQUENCE*, as a neceffary mean for defend-
ing THE RIGHTS OF THE PEOPLE, and for enforcing
good Counfels."   ROLLIN.

Publifhed according to Act of Congrefs.

Bofton:
Printed by MANNING & LORING;
For the *AUTHOR*, No. 44, for DAVID WEST, No. 56,
and for JOHN WEST, No. 75, CORNHILL.
MAY, 1797.

The Columbian Orator, 1797, opened Frederick's eyes to the possibility of freedom. He later wrote, "Liberty!...it looked from every star...and moved in every storm."

9

Broken?

Freedom became farther away than ever for Frederick when Aaron Anthony and Lucretia Auld died. Frederick then became the property of Lucretia's husband, Thomas. Frederick was sent to him when he was 15 years old. Thomas owned a store and farm near the Lloyd plantation. Thomas sent Frederick to a man named Edward Covey "to be broken."

Edward worked Frederick from dawn to dark. He beat him every week. One day, Frederick **summoned** the inner strength to fight back. Covey never touched him again.

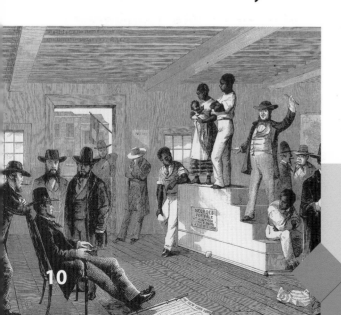

Slaves were treated cruelly. They were often whipped or sold.

This picture shows Frederick when he was about 20 years old. It is probably the earliest picture of him.

Frederick was sent to a third farm. He tried to escape but was caught. Thomas sent him back to Baltimore, where Frederick worked in the shipyards as a **caulker**. He also attended meetings of the East Baltimore Mutual Improvement Society, a secret **debating** club of free blacks. There, he fell in love with Anna Murray, a free black woman.

Escape to Freedom!

On September 3, 1838, Frederick dressed as a sailor and carried a friend's Seaman's Certificate. The certificate was proof that the person named on it was a free United States seaman. No one found out that the certificate didn't really belong to Frederick. He boarded a train to Delaware, then a steamboat to Philadelphia, and finally another train to New York City.

New York City around 1840 is pictured on the right. Frederick later wrote of arriving there, "I WAS A FREE MAN, and the voice of peace and joy thrilled my heart."

Frederick was free, but he had no home or money. He had to watch out for **slavehunters**. He met abolitionists who kept him safe. To protect his freedom, Frederick changed his last name. First he called himself Frederick Smith, then Frederick Stanley, and next Frederick Johnson.

Anna Murray came to New York, too. She and Frederick married and moved to Massachusetts. Here Frederick changed his name for the last time. He called himself Frederick Douglass, after the character in Sir Walter Scott's famous poem, *The Lady of the Lake*. Still, it was hard for a black man to find work.

Anna Murray (above) and Frederick married in 1838 and went on to have five children: Anna, Charles, Rosetta, Lewis, and Frederick Jr.

Frederick

A rare picture showing Frederick Douglass at an outdoor antislavery meeting held in New York around 1845.

Frederick began reading the newspaper *The Liberator*. It was written by William Lloyd Garrison, a white man who believed that slavery was wrong. In 1841, Frederick attended an **antislavery** meeting and was asked to speak. William thought Frederick had an important story to tell. He hired Frederick to speak at meetings. Frederick told white people about the lives of slaves.

Frederick spoke so well that people began to doubt that he had been a slave. Frederick decided to risk publishing his life story. If slavehunters found Frederick, they would take him back to Maryland. To protect his freedom, Frederick went to England, where he continued to speak against slavery. In 1846, two English Quakers, Anna and Ellen Richardson, organized a committee to free Frederick. Their committee raised $710.96 to pay Thomas Auld for Frederick's freedom. Quakers believed slavery was wrong.

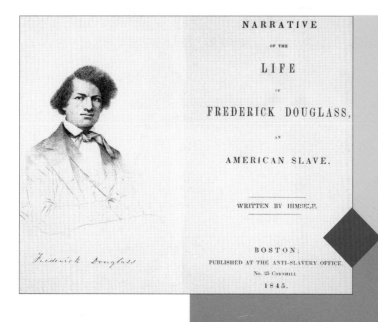

Frederick's first autobiography was published in 1845. He published two more, *My Bondage and My Freedom*, 1855, and *Life and Times of Frederick Douglass*, 1881.

Working to End Slavery

In 1847, Frederick returned to America to fight for the freedom of all slaves. He moved to Rochester, New York, where he started a newspaper called *The North Star*. The goal of his paper, and everything else Frederick said and did, was to end slavery. Frederick also spoke to help women gain the right to **vote**.

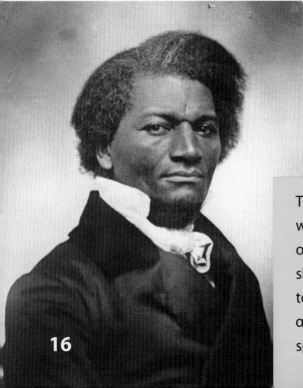

This picture of Frederick was taken in the 1840s or 1850s. The former slave who taught himself to read and write is now a respected writer, speaker, and thinker.

An advertisement published in a South Carolina newspaper in 1744 offers a reward to the person who captures the runaway slave.

RUN away, on the 3d Day of *May* laſt, a young Negro Boy, named *Joe*, this Country born, formerly belonged to Capt. *Hugh Heſt.* Whoever brings the ſaid Boy the Subſcriber at *Ediſto*, or to the Work Houſe in *Charles Town*, ſhall have 3 *l* reward. On the contrary whoever harbours the ſaid Boy, may depend upon being ſeverely proſecuted, by

Thomas Chiſham.

NOTICE OF RUNAWAY SLAVE. "CHARLESTON GAZETTE," 1744.

Within a few months of moving to Rochester, Frederick became involved with the Underground Railroad. The Underground Railroad was a system of houses and safe places where runaway slaves could hide as they made their way to northern states and Canada. Slavery was illegal in these places. Frederick's home in Rochester was close to Canada. Frederick and Anna sheltered many runaway slaves.

CHARLESTON MERCURY

EXTRA:

Passed unanimously at 1.15 o'clock, P. M., December 20th, 1860.

AN ORDINANCE

To dissolve the Union between the State of South Carolina and other States united with her under the compact entitled "The Constitution of the United States of America."

We, the People of the State of South Carolina, in Convention assembled, do declare and ordain, and it is hereby declared and ordained,

That the Ordinance adopted by us in Convention, on the twenty-third day of May, in the year of our Lord one thousand seven hundred and eighty-eight, whereby the Constitution of the United States of America was ratified, and also, all Acts and parts of Acts of the General Assembly of this State, ratifying amendments of the said Constitution, are hereby repealed; and that the union now subsisting between South Carolina and other States, under the name of "The United States of America," is hereby dissolved.

THE

UNION

IS

DISSOLVED!

A poster in which South Carolina declares that it is no longer a part of the United States. Other southern states soon followed.

In March, 1861, Abraham Lincoln became president. He **opposed** the spread of slavery. South Carolina, Georgia, Florida, Mississippi, Alabama, Louisiana, and Texas **seceded** from the United States and formed their own government. They wanted to keep slavery legal. On April 12, 1861, the **Civil War** began.

For abolitionists, the war was about slavery. If the North (the **Union**) won, slavery would end. If the South (the **Confederacy**) won, slavery would continue. In his newspaper and speeches, Frederick asked Lincoln to free all slaves so Union armies could gain thousands of strong black soldiers. On January 1, 1863, Lincoln issued the Emancipation Proclamation, which freed slaves in states that were fighting against the Union.

This picture from a New York magazine shows freed slaves joining Union forces in North Carolina during the Civil War.

Lewis (left) and Charles (right) Douglass fought for the Union in the 54th Massachusetts Regiment, a famous army unit of black volunteers known for their bravery.

The Emancipation Proclamation also stated that healthy freed slaves could join Union armies. Frederick was asked to **recruit** black soldiers. He recruited two of his sons, Lewis and Charles, and many other black men.

Black soldiers were paid less than white soldiers. They received less training, and their weapons were of lesser quality. Black soldiers captured by Confederate armies were often shot.

Frederick and Lincoln met in 1863 and 1864. They discussed Frederick's concerns about the treatment of black soldiers and Lincoln's fear that the North might lose the war. But, on April 9, 1865, the Confederacy **surrendered**, and slavery ended. Tragically, on April 14, President Lincoln was shot and killed by John Wilkes Booth. Booth hated Lincoln for ending slavery.

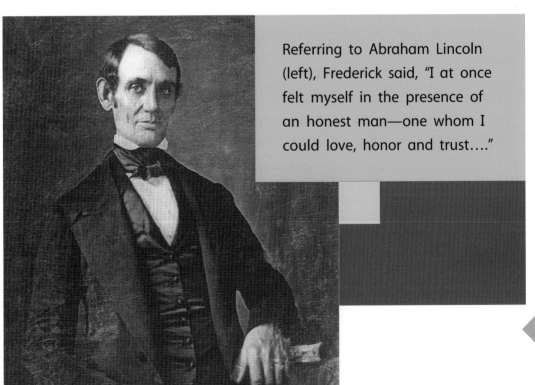

Referring to Abraham Lincoln (left), Frederick said, "I at once felt myself in the presence of an honest man—one whom I could love, honor and trust...."

Fighting for Rights

Frederick was 47 years old when the Civil War ended. He thought about retiring, but blacks still needed a leader. They had trouble finding jobs, and they were poorly paid. Many had nowhere to live. In the South, freed slaves weren't treated much better than slaves had been. Many whites did not understand these new problems. Slavery was over. What more was needed?

The Ku Klux Klan marches through Washington, D.C., in 1926. The organization was formed in 1866 to scare blacks from trying to gain equal rights.

Frederick wanted blacks to be able to vote. The new president, Andrew Johnson, did not agree. Frederick had a new battle.

He traveled, speaking to gain support for blacks' voting rights. In 1866, blacks gained citizenship when the 13th **Amendment** was

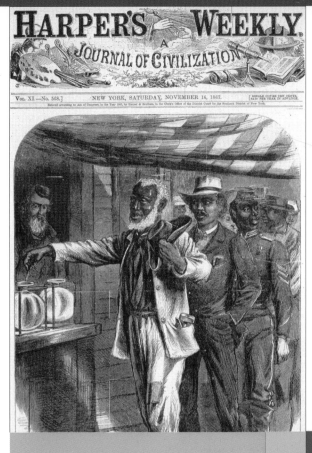

HARPER'S WEEKLY. A JOURNAL OF CIVILIZATION

Vol. XI.—No. 568.] NEW YORK, SATURDAY, NOVEMBER 16, 1867. [SINGLE COPIES TEN CENTS.

This picture from 1867 shows African Americans voting.

passed. In many states, they also gained the right to vote. In 1870, the 15th Amendment became part of the United States Constitution. It guaranteed every black man the right to vote in every state.

23

African Americans were still treated unfairly every day. Frederick continued to travel and speak about improvements for African Americans. If he was treated badly in a hotel or a restaurant because he was black, he spoke and wrote about it. He also owned and ran *The National Era*, a newspaper that reported the achievements of black Americans.

In 1877, President Rutherford B. Hayes asked Frederick to uphold the law in Washington, D.C., as **marshal.** Here, Frederick is pictured in his office at City Hall.

Helen Pitts (left) was Frederick's second wife. Many people were angry when Frederick, who had worked so hard for black people, married a white woman.

In the 1870s and 1880s, Frederick held several government jobs. In 1877, he returned to the places where he had been a slave. He visited his former master, Thomas Auld. They talked, and Frederick forgave Thomas.

In 1882, Frederick's wife, Anna, died. In 1884, Frederick married Helen Pitts, a white woman. Frederick loved Helen. He saw nothing wrong with their marriage and neither did she.

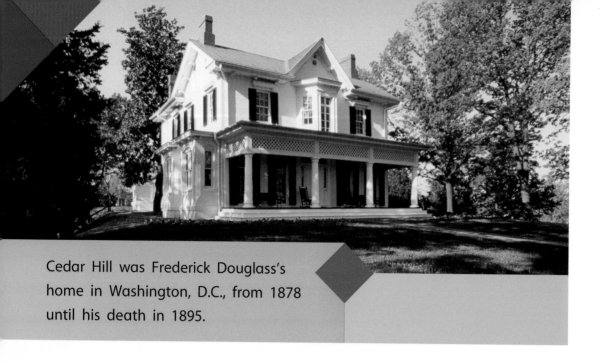

Cedar Hill was Frederick Douglass's home in Washington, D.C., from 1878 until his death in 1895.

On February 20, 1895, Frederick Douglass died of a heart attack in Washington, D.C. He was buried in Mount Hope Cemetery in Rochester, New York, beside his first wife, Anna, and his daughter, Annie. (Annie had died just before her 11th birthday in 1860.) Frederick was survived by his children, Rosetta, Lewis, Frederick, and Charles; his wife, Helen; and many grandchildren. When his second wife, Helen, died, she was buried on the other side of Frederick.

Frederick Douglass is an American hero. He was born a slave, but he never allowed anyone to own his mind. He spent his life fighting for freedom and equality, not only for himself, but for all men and women in America. He spoke out for what he believed in, no matter what the consequences, and he never gave up.

Frederick Douglass is pictured here later in life. Frederick Douglass is proof that anything is possible and that one person can make a great difference in the world.

Important Dates in Frederick's Life

1818   Frederick is born in Maryland.

1824   Frederick is sent to work as a slave on Colonel Lloyd's plantation.

1826   Frederick is sent to Baltimore to live with Hugh and Sophia Auld.

Age 15   **1833**   Frederick became a slave for Thomas Auld.

1834   Frederick is sent to Edward Covey.

1838   September—Frederick escapes to New York and freedom. He marries Anna Murray. He changes his last name to Douglass.

1841   Frederick attends his first antislavery convention and makes his first speech.

Age 25   **1845**   Frederick's first biography, *Narrative of the Life of Frederick Douglass: An American Slave, Written by Himself* is published. Frederick travels to England.

1846   Two English Quakers buy Frederick's freedom from Thomas Auld. Frederick returns to the United States and begins publishing *The North Star* newspaper.

Age 37   **1855**   Frederick publishes autobiography, *My Bondage and My Freedom.*

1860   Frederick returns to the United States. His daughter, Annie, dies.

1861   The Civil War begins (ends 1865).

1870   The 15th Amendment is ratified, guaranteeing all black men the right to vote.

Age 59   **1877**   Frederick becomes the marshal of Washington, D.C.

1881   He publishes autobiography, *Life and Times of Frederick Douglass.*

1882   Frederick's wife Anna Murray Douglass dies.

1884   Frederick marries Helen Pitts.

1895   Frederick Douglass dies at his home in Washington, D.C.

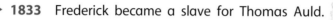

More about Black Soldiers in the Civil War

During the Civil War, about 179,000 black men fought for the Union army in about 500 battles. They made up about 10 percent of the Union army. Another 19,000 served in the navy. These military units were segregated, meaning that black men did not fight alongside white men in the same unit. Instead, black soldiers and white soldiers belonged to separate units. However, the black units were usually led by white officers.

Storming Fort Wagner, July 18, 1863. The 54th Massachusetts Regiment, the first African-American unit in the United States Army, storms Fort Wagner during the Civil War.

Some black soldiers were runaway slaves from the South. Others were free men from the North, like Frederick Douglass's sons. Lewis and Charles Douglass were among the first black men to enlist in the first black unit—the Massachusetts 54th Regiment. This unit fought in the battle at Fort Wagner, South Carolina, on July 18, 1863, one of the most well-known battles of the Civil War. More than 200 black soldiers died in another famous battle at Fort Pillow, Tennessee. The black soldiers at Fort Pillow had apparently surrendered to the Confederate army, but the Confederate soldiers killed the black soldiers anyway.

One of the most successful black units was the 1st Kansas Colored Volunteers. The men in this unit fought courageously, winning many battles. Another black unit, Company E, 4th United States Colored Infantry, was stationed in Washington, D.C., to guard the capital city. About 40,000 black soldiers died during the war, 30,000 from infection or disease. After the Civil War, President Lincoln credited the participation of African Americans in the Union forces with tipping the scales toward victory for the Union.

Glossary

amendment—a change. The Fifteenth Amendment was a change to the Constitution of the United States. It guaranteed all citizens, regardless of their race or skin color, the right to vote.

antislavery—against or hostile to the idea of slavery

caulker—someone who seals seams, cracks, or spaces in a boat or other object so the object won't leak

Civil War—the war that occurred in the United States from 1861 to 1865 between the northern and southern states

Confederate—refers to those southern states that broke away from the United States and fought for slavery and against the Union during the Civil War

debating—the act of discussing or formally arguing both sides of an issue

marshal—an officer responsible for making sure that the courts properly prosecute criminals

oppose—to be against

plantation—a large farm with a large house in which the owners live; the farm is usually worked by laborers who live nearby. During times of slavery, slaves worked the land.

recruit—to secure the services of, or to enroll as members

secede—to withdraw from an organization

slavehunters—people who captured runaway slaves, usually to receive the reward offered for their capture; they returned the runaway slaves to the slaves' owners.

summon—to call forth

surrender—to give up completely to the power of another

trough—a long, shallow container, usually placed on the ground and used for feeding animals

Union—refers to those states that remained loyal to the United States government during the Civil War

vote—to declare one's opinion toward a person or issue during an election

To Learn More

▶ **Read these books:**

Adler, David A. *A Picture Book of Frederick Douglass*. New York: Holiday House, October, 1995.

Becker, Helaine. *Frederick Douglass*. Blackbirch Marketing, September, 2001.

Miller, William. *Frederick Douglass—The Last Days of Slavery*. New York: Lee & Low Books, Inc., 1995.

Schraff, Anne E. *Frederick Douglass: Speaking Out Against Slavery*. Enslow Publishers, Inc., July 2002.

Weidt, Maryann N. *Voice of Freedom, A Story About Frederick Douglass*. Lerner Publishing Group, 2001.

▶ **Look up these Web sites:**

America's Library: Douglass's Escape From Slavery

http://www.americasstory.gov/cgi-bin/page.cgi/aa/activists/douglass/escape_1
Visit the Library of Congress web site to learn more about Frederick Douglass's escape from slavery in Maryland to freedom in New York.

America's Library: Douglass's Role in the Civil War

http://www.americasstory.gov/cgi-bin/page.cgi/aa/activists/douglass/war_1
You can also learn more about the roles that Frederick Douglass and his sons played in the Civil War at the Library of Congress web site.

Frederick Douglass National Histric Site

http://www.nps.gov/frdo/freddoug.html
Visit the Frederick Douglass National Historic Site, the official government web site of the Frederick Douglass National Historic Site in Washington, D.C., to learn more about Frederick and see a picture of his home.

▶ **Key Internet search terms:**

Frederick Douglass, slavery, Civil War, abolitionist

Index